W9-COA-059

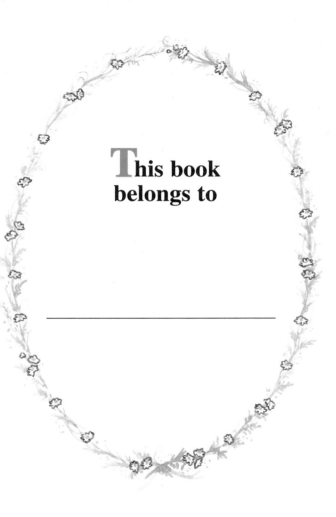

This book
belongs to

_____

Bible Wisdom for PRESCHOOLERS

Written and Illustrated by
Kathy Arbuckle

BARBOUR
PUBLISHING, INC.

Uhrichsville, Ohio

© MCMXCVII by Barbour Publishing, Inc.

ISBN 1-57748-086-4

All rights reserved. No part of this publication may be reproduced or transmitted in any form or by any means without written permission of the publisher.

Scripture quotations are from the KING JAMES VERSION of the Bible.

Published by Barbour Publishing, Inc.
P.O. Box 719
Uhrichsville, Ohio 44683
http://www.barbourbooks.com

 Member of the
Evangelical Christian
Publishers Association

Printed in Hong Kong.

For the
LORD giveth
wisdom: out of his mouth
cometh knowledge and
understanding.

PROVERBS 2:6

*For
Christina
and her
sunshine
smile.*

Bible Wisdom for Preschoolers

The fear of the LORD is the beginning of knowledge: but fools despise wisdom and instruction.

Proverbs 1:7

God's special book, the Bible, talks about the "fear of God." "Fearing God" doesn't mean that we should be afraid of God. It means that we should have much respect for God, that we should talk about, talk to, and think of Him as the most important One in the whole world, the whole universe! We should give Him all of our love and learn all that we can about Him. Then we will begin to know true wisdom.

What can God teach you today?

Bible Wisdom for Preschoolers

My son, hear the instruction of thy father, and forsake not the law of thy mother.

Proverbs 1:8

You know that your mommy and daddy are much older and bigger than you and that they know a lot of things. God has given you to your parents so they can take good care of you and teach you the things you need to grow up to be happy and strong. Sometimes they tell you what to do because they know what is best for you and they love you. God loves you, too, and He wants you to obey your parents.

What can God teach you today? 11

Bible Wisdom for Preschoolers

My son, if sinners entice thee, consent thou not.

Proverbs 1:10

Some people in the world don't love God and don't want to please Him. Instead they do bad things. Many times they will want you to do bad things, too. God says you should not listen to them. Because you love God, you should do what is right, and do the things that make God happy, not sad. Maybe others will see the good things you do and they will want to love God, too.

What can God teach you today? 13

Bible Wisdom for Preschoolers

But whoso hearkeneth unto me
shall dwell safely.

Proverbs 1:33

"Look out!" That is what Joshua said
when he saw the red wagon rolling
towards his friend Sam. Sam heard the
warning and got safely out of the way.
The Bible, God's special book, tells us
what God says. If you listen to God's
Word and do what it says, God will do
what is best for you. Just like a caring
friend, God is always there to
protect you.

Bible Wisdom for Preschoolers

For the L<small>ORD</small> giveth wisdom: out of his mouth cometh knowledge and understanding.

Proverbs 2:6

Books are fun to look at and read. You can learn a lot from them. God has His own book called the Bible. In the Bible God has told us many things that help us to live the way He wants us to. You see, God knows everything. Everything He says is right and good, so if you listen to His words, you will learn what is right and good, too.

Trust in the LORD with all thine heart; and lean not unto thine own understanding. In all thy ways acknowledge him, and he shall direct thy paths.

Proverbs 3:5,6

One morning Meghan thought she could pour the juice herself for her breakfast, so she didn't ask for any help. Meghan didn't know that it would be so hard to pour. Meghan made a big mess. God wants to be in your life everyday. He is there to help you and teach you how to do your best. So talk to Him. Learn about Him. And never be afraid to ask for help.

What can God teach you today?   19

Bible Wisdom for Preschoolers

Honor the L<small>ORD</small> with thy substance, and with the first fruits of all thine increase: So shall thy barns be filled with plenty.

Proverbs 3:9,10

Everything you have was given to you by God. He made everything and owns the whole world and all that is in it. Because He has been so good to us we should give back to Him some of what He has given us. When you give to God you show Him that you love Him and that He is very important to you. After all, God has given you His very best.

Bible Wisdom for Preschoolers

For whom the LORD loveth he cor-
recteth; even as a father the son in
whom he delighteth.

Proverbs 3:12

God told Jonah to go tell the people to
stop being wicked, but Jonah didn't
want to obey. So he sailed away on a
boat. While on the boat, a bad storm
came and a big fish swallowed Jonah. It
took three days in the fish's belly for
Jonah to decide to obey God. The fish
spit Jonah out. Jonah told the people
what God had said and a wonderful
thing happened: the wicked people
changed and decided to love God!
Sometimes, you get in trouble for not
obeying your parents, but
they love you and they
want to protect you.

Bible Wisdom for Preschoolers

Happy is the man that findeth wisdom, and the man that getteth understanding.

Proverbs 3:13

Sarah has been learning about God. She has learned that God is all-powerful; He is everywhere; He knows everything; and He loves her very, very much. He loves her so much that He gave His Son, Jesus, to be her Savior. Knowing all of these wonderful things makes Sarah happy. Like Sarah, the more you know about God and His wisdom, the happier you will be.

What can God teach you today? 25

Bible Wisdom for Preschoolers

The LORD by wisdom hath founded the earth; by understanding hath he established the heavens.

Proverbs 3:19

Look at all that is around you. There are animals of every shape and color. They walk, run, swim, or even fly. The plants, trees, and flowers grow and bloom in every color of the rainbow. The earth itself is amazing with its tall mountains, sandy beaches, grassy meadows, and rushing rivers. At night the stars and the moon shine brightly overhead. All of these awesome things were made by God. His knowledge is greater than anyone's.

Bible Wisdom for Preschoolers

Withhold not good from them to whom it is due, when it is in the power of thine hand to do it.

Proverbs 3:27

Sometimes a job is too big for one person to do alone, but two people make it easier. God is pleased when He sees you help someone else. It makes Him happy when you do something good for another person. Even little things like helping to set the table for dinner or helping the neighbor lady rake up the leaves are important ways you can do good for others. When you are a helper you are sharing God's love.

Bible Wisdom for Preschoolers

Devise not evil against thy neighbor, seeing he dwelleth securely
by thee.

Proverbs 3:29

Do you know your neighbors? Are they
your friends? God's Son, Jesus, said we
should love our neighbors, all of them.
It does not matter if they are rich or
poor, young or old, short or tall, boys
or girls, or what color skin they have.
We should be friendly to all our
neighbors because God made them
and He loves them.

Bible Wisdom for Preschoolers

For wisdom is better than rubies; and all the things that may be desired are not to be compared to it.

Proverbs 8:11

Wisdom is having knowledge and knowing how to use it to please God. Imagine that you found a treasure chest filled with jewels and gold. That treasure would be very valuable, wouldn't it? But God's wisdom is far more valuable than some pretty rocks and shiny metal. Wisdom helps you to live a life that pleases God. And when others see your life they will want to love God, too. Treasures only last for a little while, but God's love lasts FOREVER.

What can God teach you today?   33

Bible Wisdom for Preschoolers

The mouth of a righteous man is a well of life.

Proverbs 10:11

Every living thing needs water to live: people, plants, animals, and especially fish! Many people get their water from a well. A well is a deep hole in the ground that reaches cool, pure water trapped in the rocks. Some farmers use well water for their animals and fields. So you can see how a well is "life." People who love God can be like "wells of life." They talk about God and share God's love with others. They don't hurt people with mean words, but use their words to please God. You can be a "well of life" for someone today!

Bible Wisdom for Preschoolers

The way of the LORD is strength to the upright.

Proverbs 10:29

The Bible tells about a young man named David. One day he went to bring food to his big brothers who were soldiers at a battle. While there, David found himself fighting a giant named Goliath. Now David was still a boy, so he was small compared to Goliath, but he prayed for God to give him the strength to defeat the giant. The Lord answered David's prayer! God will be your strength, too. All you have to do is ask Him for help and He will be there for you.

Bible Wisdom for Preschoolers

A false balance is abomination to the LORD: but a just weight is his delight.

Proverbs 11:1

One day Brian was at the market with his mother buying groceries. He helped her choose five pounds of shiny, red apples. They used the store's scale to weigh the apples and make sure that they were buying five pounds. God wants us to be honest. He wants us to always tell the truth and not lie to each other or to Him. Lies only hurt people. They never help anyone. False words make God sad and angry, but when you are truthful it makes Him happy.

Bible Wisdom for Preschoolers

Where no counsel is, the people fall: but in the multitude of counsellors there is safety.

Proverbs 11:14

Lindsay wanted to ride her bike to her friend Bonnie's house. Lindsay asked her mommy if it was okay and then used the map Bonnie had made to show her the way. The directions made it easy for Lindsay to find Bonnie's house. Without them, Lindsay would have gotten lost. It is good to ask for help when you don't know about something. Your family and friends will be glad to help you. And, of course, God is always there to give you His help, too. Just ask Him.

What can God teach you today?   41

Bible Wisdom for Preschoolers

A righteous man regardeth the life of his beast: but the tender mercies of the wicked are cruel.

Proverbs 12:10

You can see Joey filling up his dog's water dish. Joey loves Speckles, his dog, and wants to take very good care of him. He makes sure Speckles has everything he needs to be safe and healthy. We should all do our best to take extra good care of our animals. God made all the puppies, kitties, birds, lizards, mice, horses, and every other animal. They are His gifts to us to care for and love.

Bible Wisdom for Preschoolers

The way of a fool is right in his own eyes: but he that hearkeneth unto counsel is wise.

Proverbs 12:15

Sam crashed his bicycle after riding it over a big jump. Sam's friend Johnny had told him not to ride over it. Johnny said, "It's too big, Sam! You might get hurt!" Sam now knows that he should have listened to his friend. Johnny only wanted to protect Sam. Sometimes your parents or friends tell you not to do something. You should think carefully about what they say and use their words to help you make a smart decision. They love you and only want what is best for you.

What can God teach you today?

Bible Wisdom for Preschoolers

He that speaketh truth sheweth forth righteousness: but a false witness deceit.

Proverbs 12:17

Candace likes the lamp in her room. It makes the whole room bright. When you tell the truth you are like that lamp. Everyone around you can see God's goodness and love by watching how good you are to others. So always be honest with your family, friends, and everybody you know, especially God. It makes Him smile to see you shine with truthfulness.

What can God teach you today?

Bible Wisdom for Preschoolers

There is that speaketh like the piercings of a sword: but the tongue of the wise is health.

Proverbs 12:18

When someone says mean words to you it makes you feel bad, doesn't it? Your feelings are hurt and sometimes you might even cry. But when somebody says nice things to you and tells you good things, things they know will help you, that makes you happy. You feel good when you know people care about you and that they are there whenever you need them. Use your words to make others happy and God will be glad, too.

What can God teach you today? 49

Bible Wisdom for Preschoolers

In the way of righteousness is life: and in the pathway thereof there is no death.

Proverbs 12:28

Imagine a pathway that leads to a beautiful city where the streets are paved with gold. The King who rules over that city is loving and very kind to all of His subjects. The people of this city wear crowns of gold with jewels and are never hungry or sad or sick. They live forever in this wonderful place. This is what God has for you when you follow Him and obey Him. When you believe in God's Son, Jesus, you will be walking on the pathway to heaven and life forever with the loving King.

The soul of the sluggard desireth, and hath nothing: but the soul of the diligent shall be made fat.

Proverbs 13:4

One day Kevin saw a toy dump truck at the toy store. He did not have enough money to buy it, so he asked his parents if he could do extra jobs to earn the money. It took some time and some hard work, but soon he had enough money to buy the shiny, new truck. Because Kevin was willing to work extra, he was able to get what he wanted. If he had been lazy, do you think he would have been able to buy his new toy?

There is that maketh himself rich, yet hath nothing: there is that maketh himself poor, yet hath great riches.

Proverbs 13:7

Long ago, King Solomon was the richest man in the world. He had so many jewels that he could never wear them all. His stables were filled with many fine horses and he lived in a grand palace. However, these riches did not make him happy. He was only truly happy when he was loving God with his whole heart. Even if King Solomon did not have a single penny, he still would have been happy as long as he loved and obeyed God. God's love is the greatest treasure you can have.

Bible Wisdom for Preschoolers

He that walketh with wise men shall be wise: but a companion of fools shall be destroyed.

Proverbs 13:20

Amy and Jennifer are very best friends. They both like to play with dolls and toy horses. Blue is their favorite color and they both like the same flavor of ice cream. But most important, they both love God. The two friends like to do what is right and share the love of God with each other and with their friends and families. Their friendship grows as they learn more and more about the Lord together.

What can God teach you today?

Bible Wisdom for Preschoolers

He that is soon angry dealeth foolishly.

Proverbs 14:17

Have you ever heard that someone has a "bad temper"? That means that the person gets very mad very easily. Do you like to be around somebody like that? It hurts your feelings when a person yells at you and is grumpy towards you. Being angry usually does not solve any problems, but instead makes them worse. God tells us not to have a bad temper, but to use kind words. He knows that is the best way to work out a problem.

A sound heart is the life of the flesh: but envy the rottenness of the bones.

Proverbs 14:30

Justin had a blue bicycle with training wheels. But Marty had a new, red bike with a headlight. Justin wished that he had Marty's bike instead of his. He was sad all the time because he thought the bike he had was not good enough. Justin was jealous. Soon he realized that God had given him his bicycle and that he should be thankful for it. Justin stopped wasting his time feeling bad and soon was out with Marty. They rode their nice bikes and had fun together. That made God happy.

What can God teach you today?

Bible Wisdom for Preschoolers

He that oppresseth the poor
reproacheth his Maker: but he that
honoureth him hath mercy on the
poor.

Proverbs 14:31

There are many poor people in the
world who don't have much of anything.
God's Son, Jesus, cares about the poor
and told us to care about them, too,
because He loves them. It pleases God
when He sees you share with someone
who might not have what you have.
Besides, it is much more fun to fly a
kite with a friend than to fly it all
by yourself!

Bible Wisdom for Preschoolers

A soft answer turneth away wrath: but grievous words stir up anger.

Proverbs 15:1

Kaitlyn wanted her puppy, Goldie, to come to her, so she shouted, "Goldie!" in a loud voice. The dog was afraid and did not come. Kaitlyn became angry and yelled louder at the frightened puppy. The little dog ran farther away. Finally, Kaitlyn thought, "How would Jesus call my doggie?" Sweetly, with a gentle voice, Kaitlyn called her puppy. Goldie's tail began to wag and she ran right into Kaitlyn's waiting arms for a loving hug. People like soft words, too, because they make love grow.

The eyes of the L‍ORD are in every place, beholding the evil and the good.

Proverbs 15:3

Did you know that God is everywhere all of the time? He is so big and so awesome that He can be all over the universe at the same time. That is a good thing to think about as you go through your day. Always remember that God is right there to help you make good decisions and do the right things. We want to please God with everything we do and say all the day long.

The LORD is far from the wicked: but he heareth the prayer of the righteous.

Proverbs 15:29

Nathan's great-grandma lives far away in another state. It is too far to visit by car, but the telephone lets them talk together as if they lived very close. Every Saturday morning, Nathan's great-grandma calls to talk to him. She likes to be able to tell him that she loves him. Your love for God makes you close to Him and when you are close to Him, He will hear your prayers. You can talk to Him anytime without even having to use the telephone!

What can God teach you today?

Bible Wisdom for Preschoolers

How much better is it to get wisdom than gold! and to get understanding rather to be chosen than silver!

Proverbs 16:16

It is better to have wisdom and do what is right than to have all of the money in the world. Would God be happy if you were very rich, but you did not love Him? He would rather have your love even if you were the poorest of poor. You are more precious to Him than all the diamonds in the world! Knowing God and doing what He says is worth far more than the greatest treasures of gold and silver.

What can God teach you today? 71

Bible Wisdom for Preschoolers

The highway of the upright is to depart from evil: he that keepeth his way preserveth his soul.

Proverbs 16:17

Imagine you are standing on a road trying to decide which way to go. If you go one way, the road leads to a smelly, dark garbage dump. But if you travel on that road the other way, it will lead you to a wonderful place where the air is filled with sweet music and laughter, and bright light shines all around you. Which way would you go? God says you should choose the good way, the way that goes far away from evil. As you travel with Him He will lead you and keep you safe in His love.

Bible Wisdom for Preschoolers

Pleasant words are as an honey-comb, sweet to the soul, and health to the bones.

Proverbs 16:24

Brianne's favorite fruit is juicy water-melon. She likes the sweet taste and how it crunches when she takes a bite. God made the watermelon so it is full of vitamins and other healthy things to help Brianne grow up big and strong. The Bible says that nice words are sweet. They are good for us to say and good for us to hear, too. Pleasant words help us to be healthy, happy children of God.

Bible Wisdom for Preschoolers

A friend loveth at all times, and a brother is born for adversity.

Proverbs 17:17

Amanda and Isabel are best friends. They do everything together. But when Amanda broke her leg falling off her trampoline, she could not go outside to play anymore until her leg healed. That didn't bother Isabel. She came over every day to visit her friend Amanda and play with her. Amanda had so much fun that she forgot all about her broken leg. God wants us to be good friends ALL of the time, in bad times and good.

What can God teach you today?

Bible Wisdom for Preschoolers

The name of the LORD is a strong tower: the righteous runneth into it, and is safe.

Proverbs 18:10

Long ago, during Bible times, there were places called "cities of refuge." If someone was in trouble with another person, they could run to one of these cities and be safe. No one could come after them to hurt them as long as they stayed in that city of refuge. God is like a city of refuge. When you are afraid you can talk to Him and He will protect you like a strong tower. God is mightier than anyone or anything. He will be your safe place.

Bible Wisdom for Preschoolers

A man that hath friends must shew himself friendly: and there is a friend that sticketh closer than a brother.

Proverbs 18:24

Michael loved to go fishing. He went many, many times to the same pond, but never caught a fish. After a while fishing wasn't fun anymore. One day a new neighbor boy asked Michael if there were any good places to fish nearby. The two boys went together once, twice, three times, four times to the pond. They never did catch any fish, but they built a wonderful friendship that lasted their whole lives long. To have a friend you have to be a friend.

Bible Wisdom for Preschoolers

The sluggard will not plow by rea-
son of the cold; therefore shall he
beg in harvest, and have nothing.

Proverbs 20:4

Once there was a farmer who was lazy.
On sunny days he might do a little work
in his field if he felt like it, but if it was
at all cold, he would not work at all.
Time went by. Spring and summer were
gone and it was harvesttime. All of the
farmer's neighbors were harvesting their
crops and storing food for the winter,
but the lazy farmer did not have any
crops to harvest. He was very hungry.
The Bible says that if we are willing to
work, we will
earn what we
need to live.

Bible Wisdom for Preschoolers

Who can say, I have made my heart clean, I am pure from my sin?

Proverbs 20:9

Benjamin likes to help wash the dishes. Now if no one washed those dishes, would they get clean all by themselves? No, they wouldn't. Someone has to get the dish soap and water and scrub them. When you do something bad you are like the dirty dishes. You can't clean away your sin by yourself. You have to be sorry and ask God to forgive you and wash away your sin. And just like the very best dishwasher, He will make you sparkling clean and pure!

Bible Wisdom for Preschoolers

Say not thou, I will recompense evil; but wait on the LORD, and he shall save thee.

Proverbs 20:22

One summer day at the beach Luke and Zachary were building sand castles. Zachary was driving his toy dump truck too fast and knocked down Luke's sand castle. Luke became angry and wanted to go knock down Zachary's sand castle, but he remembered that God says not to "get even" with anyone. God will deal with that person Himself. It is not your job. After all, God's ways are perfect. He knows best what to do.

Bible Wisdom for Preschoolers

The horse is prepared against the day of battle: but safety is of the LORD.

Proverbs 21:31

Many years ago an army's strength was measured by how many horses and soldiers it had. Each soldier would take care of his horse, train it, and even put armor on it to help protect it during battle. There were no tanks or jet planes back then. The soldier's power was his horse. God says not to put your trust in things. He is your strength and protection. God is more powerful than any army or tank or anything else in the universe, and He is on your side.

Bible Wisdom for Preschoolers

Train up a child in the way he should go: and when he is old, he will not depart from it.

Proverbs 22:6

The Bible is a wonderful book filled with the words God has said. He gave us His book so that we would know how to live with each other and how to love and serve Him. If you start learning about God when you are young, you will know so much by the time you grow up! So listen carefully to your parents, grandparents, and Bible teachers when they teach you about God. They love you and they want to see you grow up big and strong in God's love.

What can God teach you today?

Bible Wisdom for Preschoolers

Let another man praise thee, and not thine own mouth.

Proverbs 27:2

Sherman hit a home run in the baseball game. He told everyone all about how great he was and what a super home run he hit. Sherman was bragging. He was telling others how great he thinks he is. Bragging is not a good thing unless it is someone else who is bragging about you. So go ahead and tell about how good someone else is, but let another person be the one who brags about you.

Bible Wisdom for Preschoolers

He that covereth his sins shall not prosper: but whoso confesseth and forsaketh them shall have mercy.

Proverbs 28:13

Becky ate some of the cake her mommy had made for tomorrow's party. Becky knew she wasn't supposed to eat it, but she did anyway. She couldn't hide what she had done. The best thing for her to do is to tell her mommy and say she is sorry. She should pray to God, too, and tell Him she is sorry and ask Him to forgive her. Becky has learned that she should not try to hide her sins and that she is forgiven when she asks for forgiveness.

Every word of God is pure: he is a shield unto them that put their trust in him.

Proverbs 30:5